my Great day

A Day that Rhymes

Enjoy a cheerful rhyme
at any event of day.
And after some time,
Work will seem like play.

When it's time for me to get up,
It's also time to feed my pup.
I can't be late
and make him wait,
That wouldn't make him
feel too great.

fun tip

Before you jump out of bed, take a moment to make a wish. A wish for something new, a wish for someone you love.

After realizing all I had to do,
I felt rather down and tearful.
But then I found a better way,
And decided to be cheerful.

fun tip
Write a list of what you need to do to be ready for the day. Hang it behind a window or glass picture frame, and use a whiteboard marker to add a smiley face next to it when you get it done.

The pick-up

? What things need to be picked up in this picture?

I make my bed each day,
And put my toys away.
And when I look around,
Mess is nowhere
to be found.

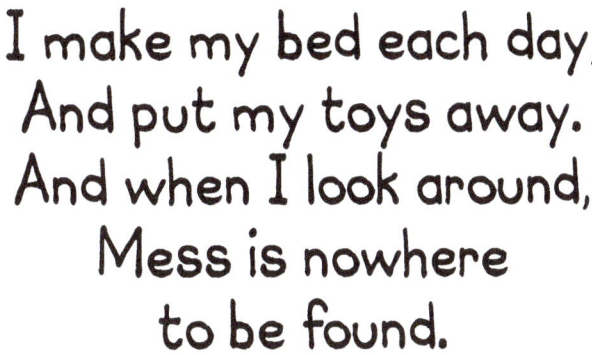

fun tip

Put on a song and pick up as many things in your room as you possibly can while it's playing. How much better does your room look now? Do you think your room needs another "pick-up" song?

Terrific teacher

? How do you treat your teacher or elders?

I'm not as big as you,
But I'm a person, too.
You talk to me with respect,
And that's how I'll answer you.

fun tip

Make a card or picture for your teacher. Give it to her as you compliment her for something. Did she brighten up with a smile? That's one way to show respect.

I fumbled and
I stumbled;
Then down, down,
down I tumbled.
But next time I can say:
"I'll try a wiser way."

fun tip
When you make a mistake, think about where you went wrong. Then think about what you will try next time, and say it out loud to 3 people.

Get it right

What helps you concentrate on your work?

I can do it right;
I can do it well.
I can finish up,
Before I say,
"farewell."

fun tip

Is it hard to concentrate? Pick an item in the room to use as a reminder to focus on your work. Every time you look at it, let it remind you of your promise.

Care for my world

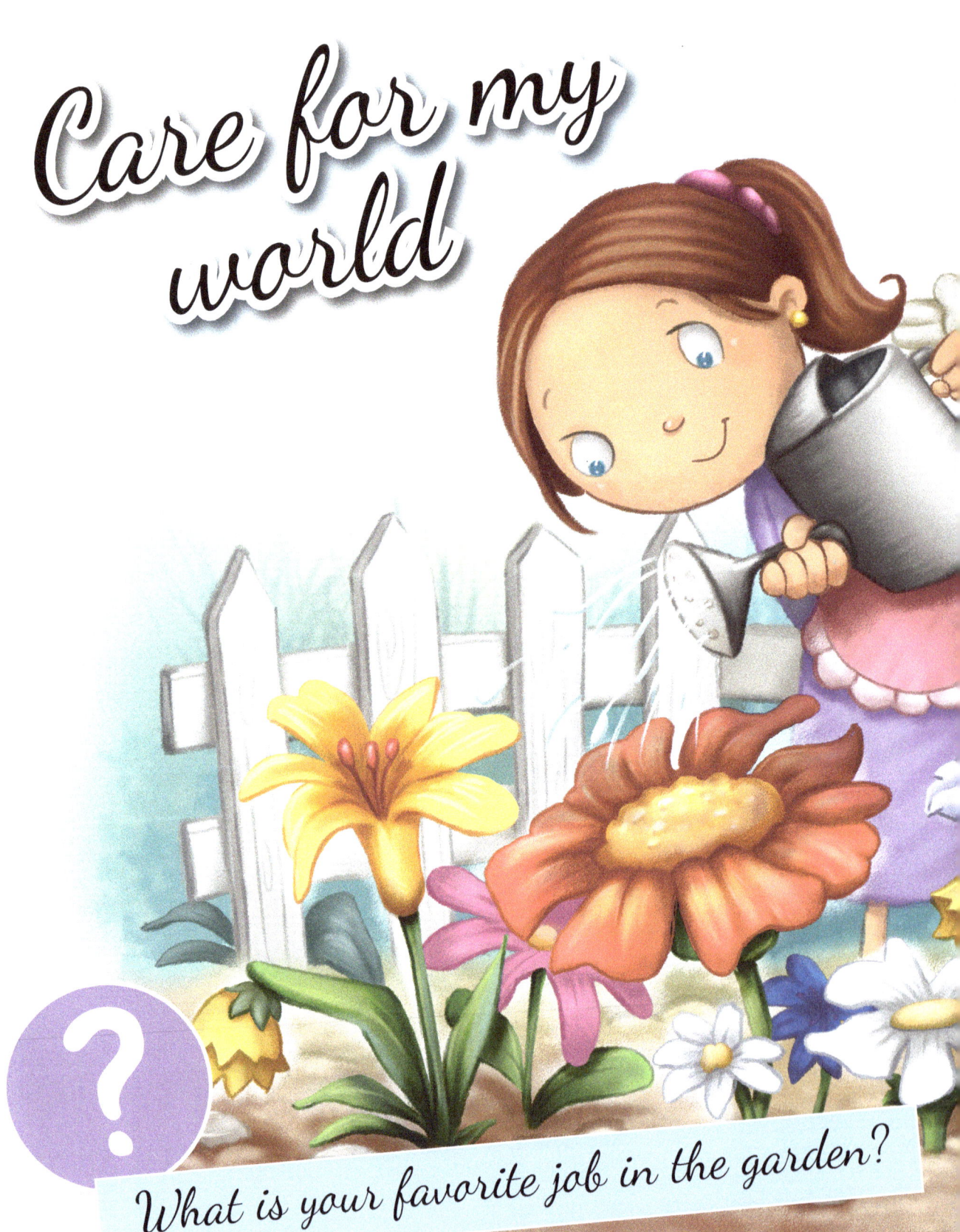

?

What is your favorite job in the garden?

Our town is not very clean.
I want to help it look more green.
So I plant some flowers to bloom.
Now our town smells like perfume.

fun tip
Cut a green sheet of paper into strips. Walk around your home and stick each strip onto the things you feel you can help tidy up or take better care of throughout your day.

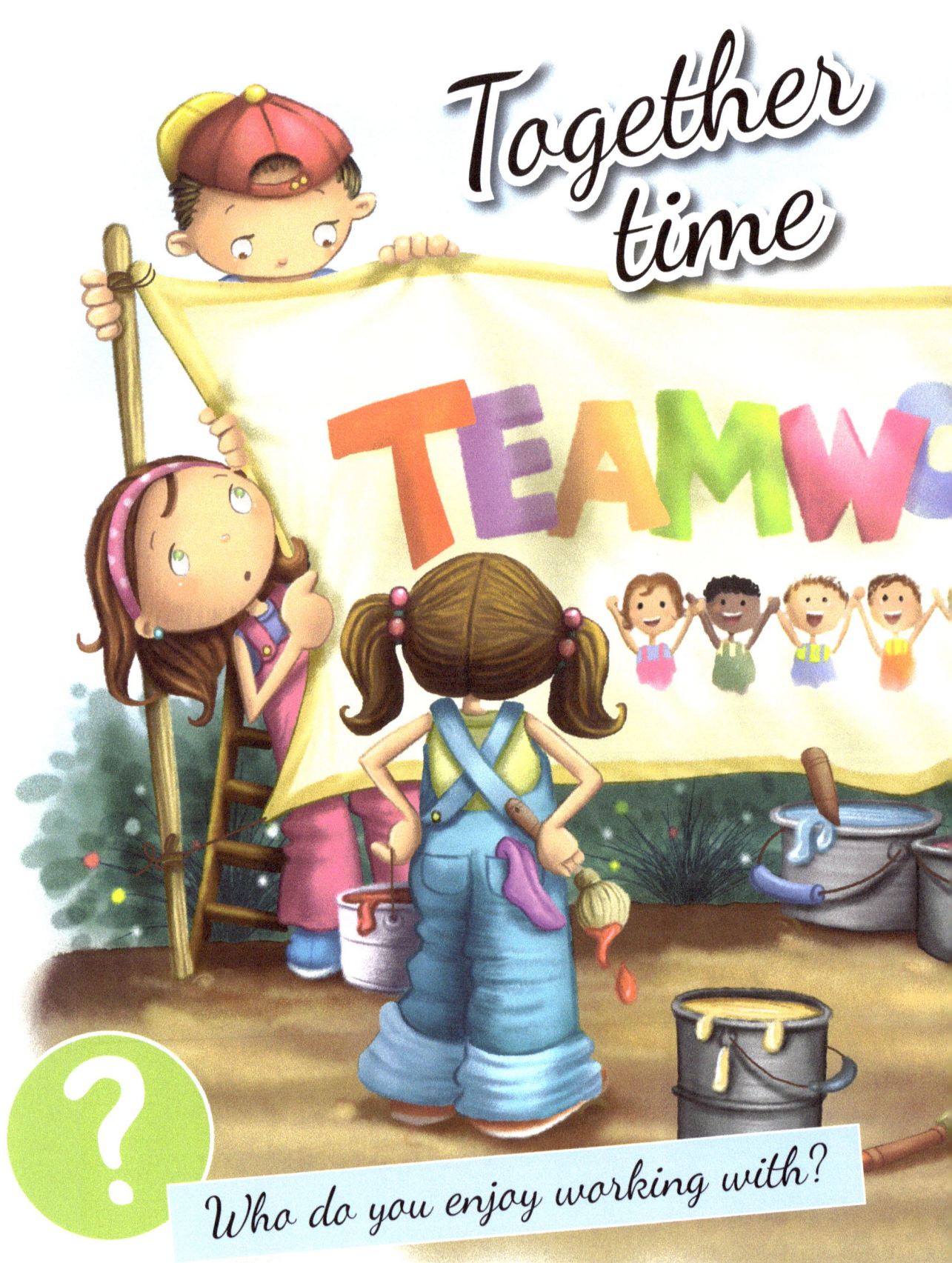

"Why don't we
prepare a show,
Our parents would
love it, you know."
They talked,
they imagined,
they planned.
When working together,
things were grand.

fun tip
With your friends or family, write out the word TEAMWORK on a sheet of paper. Think of things that require teamwork, that begins with each letter of the word.

Out for a drive

How often do you go out for a drive?

When for a drive we go,
I keep my voice real low.
I buckle up and
look outside,
And we have a
pleasant ride.

fun tip
A game to play while on a long drive: Look out the window and try to spot something that starts with the letter A. When someone calls it out, move on to the letter B. Keep going until you have gone through the whole alphabet together.

Oh, this food,
it's not so great;
I do not like it on
my plate.
But I'm told that
it's good for me,
So I will eat it
thankfully.

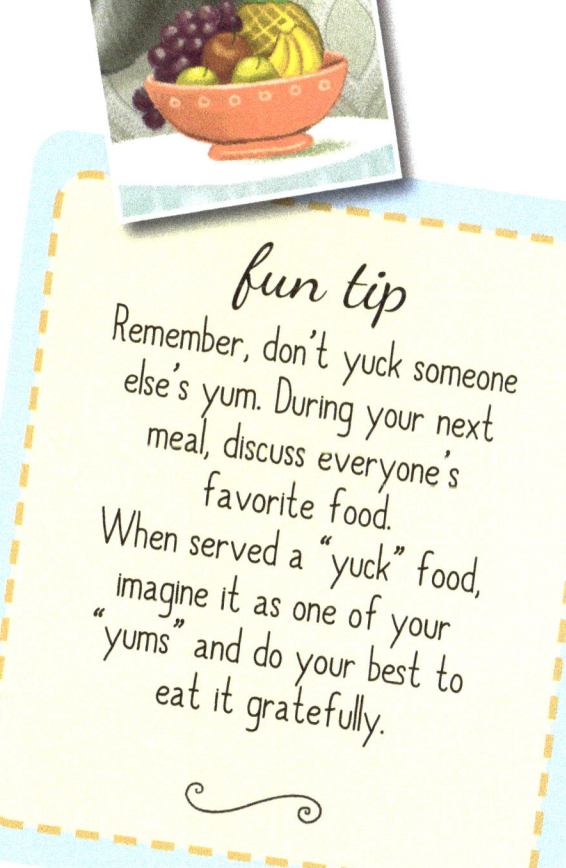

fun tip

Remember, don't yuck someone else's yum. During your next meal, discuss everyone's favorite food.
When served a "yuck" food, imagine it as one of your "yums" and do your best to eat it gratefully.

Slow it down

? When do you take your little breaks?

It gets loud
during the day,
Especially when I run
around and play.
So I take some time
to slow it down;
It helps me not to
get run down.

fun tip
Write down on little cards some quiet projects you like to do (read a book, draw a picture, do a puzzle, listen to music, etc.). Put the cards in a bowl or envelope. The next time you need an idea for a quiet activity, pick out one of the cards and do it.

The clown show

How do you like to cheer others up?

If someone is
feeling down,
And their face
has got a frown;
I sneak up and
cheer them up,
I might even use
clown makeup.

fun tip

Cut out some colored paper hearts and hide them around your room. Anytime you find one, let it remind you to do something nice for others. It could be simple like giving Mom a hug, appreciating Dad, putting something away for a sibling. But it works like magic.

When I give,
and when I share,
It shows others
that I care.
At times I have
more than I need;
So sharing is a
thoughtful deed.

fun tip

Take a cardboard box and wrap some nice paper around it, like if it was a gift. Every time you give or share with others, glue a sticker, decoration or ribbon onto it. Watch your giving box and sharing heart become more and more beautiful.

When someone makes a mistake
And causes something to break,
It's easy to get mad and yell,
But forgiving words are
better to tell.

fun tip
During dinner with your family, let everyone say "sorry" for one thing that they've done wrong to someone else. How did it feel when the other person said "I forgive you"?

Not as planned

What could be good about the rain?

When there's a lot of rain,
I'm thankful for the sun.
I like to think of things
that make me happy,
Because that's much
more fun.

fun tip
Cut pictures from magazines of things that you enjoy or like to do. Place them in a "Not as planned" jar. The next time plans change or you are disappointed, pick a picture from the jar to remind you of the good in life.

Snack treats

When do you remember to use these words?

There are two great words
That I love to use all year;
"Please" and "Thanks,"
Are pleasant to hear.

fun tip
During your next family get together, take turns to remember the last 3 "please" and "thank you's" that you heard. Then tell everyone who said it and what they said it for. Where any of those from you?

Blowing kisses from up high;
Dropping notes of cheer.
Love is something I can share,
Even from way up here.

fun tip

Take a red colored paper and cut it into plenty of small strips. Staple or tape togehter the ends of one strip and hang it onto your door handle. Every time you do something loving, loop a new strip onto it, as you create your own loving paper chain.

Helping hands

? How do you like to help others?

Hands can fix;
Hands can share.
Hands can help,
To show I care.

fun tip
Print out a coloring page and cut it in half. Give one half to your best friend to color, while you color the other half. When you're both done, glue the two parts together and you'll have a work of art made by two great friends. Hang it up as a reminder of your friendship.

Safety-smart

? How do you do your best to keep safe?

I can roll over, jump and run;
I can play and have great fun.
But I make sure that when I play,
That I am safe along the way.

fun tip

Make yourself a courage badge out of cardboard. Decorate it with bright colors and have it say "Keep up the good work!" or "Don't give up!" or "The winner!". Wear it the next time you try something new or challenging.

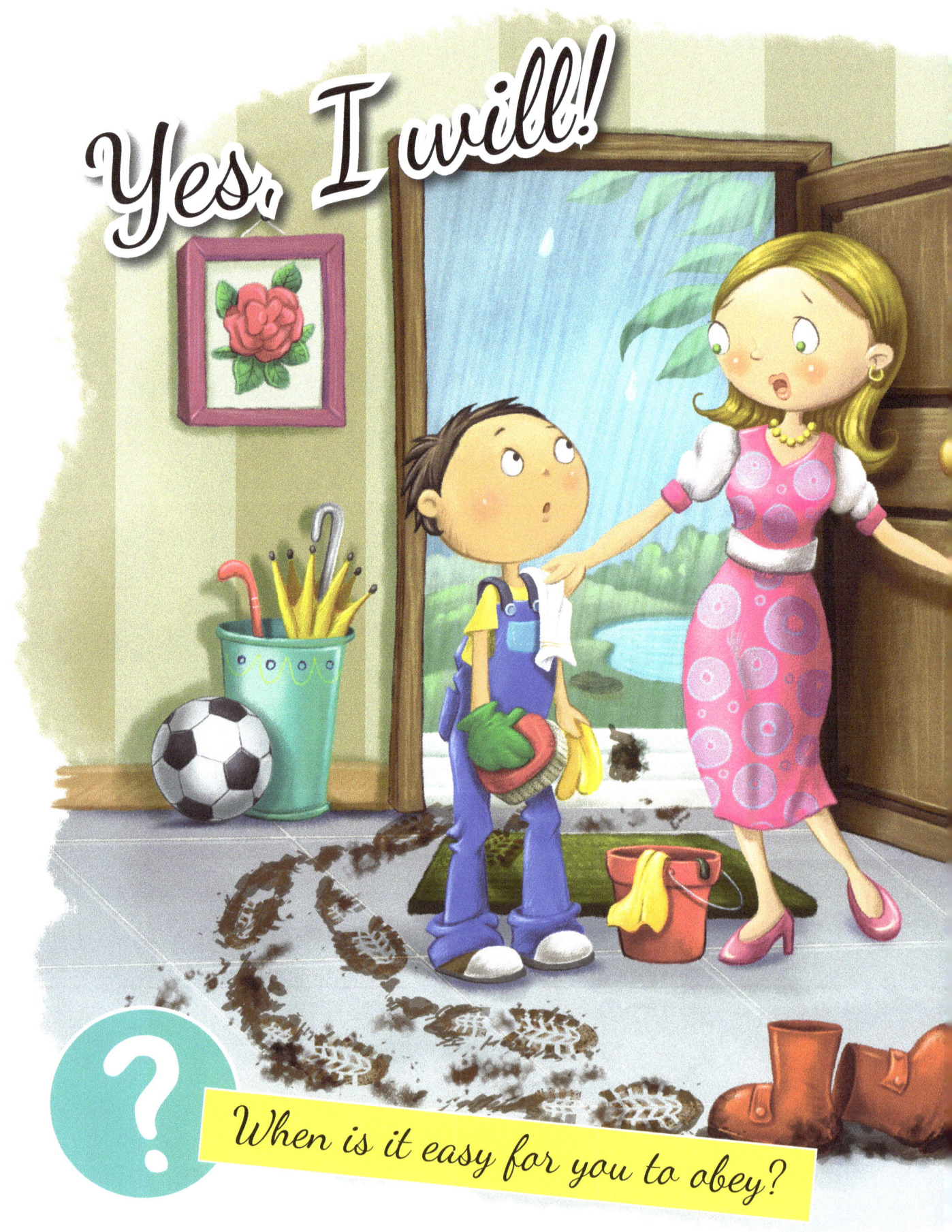

Mom asks me to clean a mess,
I smile and answer, "yes."
I keep at it till it's done;
Then I go and have some fun.

fun tip

Draw a picture of a responsibility that you would like to learn. Ask a grown up for their advice on how to do it. Each time you practice the responsibility, color one part of the picture. See if you have mastered the job by the time the picture is fully colored.

I don't know if I can do it;
Sometimes I'm afraid to try.
But everyone believes I can,
And next time, so will I.

fun tip

On a paper, using a red marker write something that you need to do but are a bit hesitant and afraid to do. Then ask family members and friends to write something positive about it, along the sides of the paper, using a green marker. Let their notes encourage and comfort you onwards.

When in a store, I can't deny
There are lots of things
I'd like to buy.
But I don't whine
when Mom insists,
That we just buy
what's on the list.

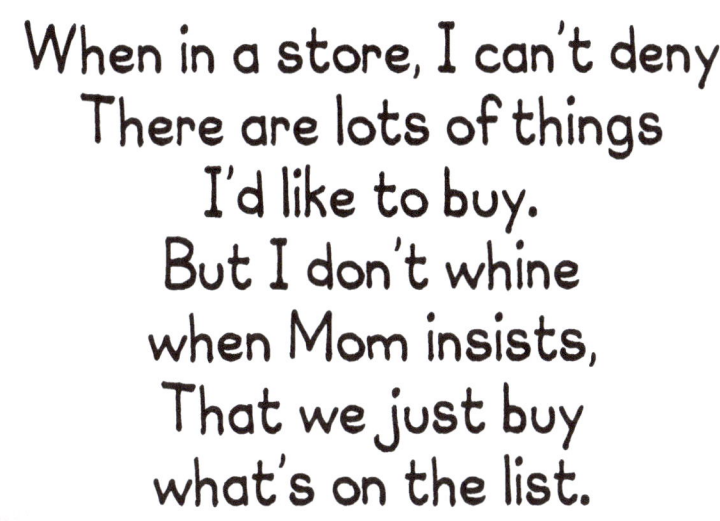

fun tip

The next time your parents go to the supermarket, ask if you can be responsible to get all the fruits or milk products or snack foods. Make a shopping list by drawing or writing the items. Get a trolley and you're ready to be a great shopper. Watch how it works to pay at the checkout counter, and then give it a try next time.

Can I help?

What is a little job in the house you like to do?

I may be small
and not so tall,
But I can be a
help to all.
The caring things
I do and say,
Make me important
every day.

fun tip

Write the days of the week onto post-its. then stick them onto objects around the house that you'd like to help take care of each day. (Ei: Monday: sink, Tuesday: broom, Wednesday: dusting, etc.) Once you've finished a job, move the post-its to your bedroom door. See if you can get all 7 jobs on the door by the end of your week.

I greet people at the door;
I greet people at the store.
I'm kind and polite
to all I meet;
I give a smile,
that's being sweet.

fun tip

When guests come for a visit, remember these simple steps:

G–GREET with a cheerful "Hello!"
U–USE hands to give a shake or hug
E–ENTER as you take their coat
S–SERVE drinks or snacks
T–TALKING with them is important

Table manners

? How are these kids using good manners?

I sit still when in my seat,
And have good manners
when I eat.
I don't let food
fall to the ground.
I consider those around.

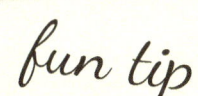

fun tip
Draw a few piglet pictures and cut them out. When poor manners are spotted at meal time, the offender is given a piglet. At the end of the meal, those without a piglet get to enjoy a dessert.

Choose your style

What do you each day, to keep yourself clean?

I keep myself nice and clean,
So that whenever I am seen;
People meet me
with delight,
Because I'm a
pleasant sight.

fun tip
Draw a picture of yourself. Go from head to toe and write what you do to keep clean next to each body part. For example: wash hair, brush hair, wash face, brush teeth, clean inside ears, take a bath, wear clean clothes, change underwear each day…. and finish at the toes.

Free time

What do you like to do in your free time?

There are many things to do.
Just look at what I drew?
I use my time wisely,
Learning makes
me happy.

fun tip
Choose one thing that you enjoy doing. Practice it during your free times, and after a while you will notice yourself getting better at it.

Swing and glide, catch and run;
Playing together is lots of fun.

I'm nice to you,
you're nice to me;
Making playtime
happy as can be.

fun tip

Place a small box or basket by your bed. Fill it with books, games or objects to use with your siblings or parents before bed as a special time together. Once you've finished using them all, collect some new items for more fun times.

When I lie down,
I close my eyes,
Or maybe look out
at the skies.
I keep quiet,
I don't make a peep,
And soon I find
that I'm fast asleep.

fun tip
While trying to fall asleep, think about the favorite things that happened today. Count how many things you are thankful for. It'll help you go to sleep with thoughts that make you smile.

Visit our website for these and other great products:
www.Kidible.eu

www.kidible.eu
By Agnes and Salem de Bezenac
Illustrated by Agnes de Bezenac
Colored by Reema S., Noviyandi W.
Copyright. All rights reserved.
Published by iCharacter Ltd. (Ireland)
Kidible is an imprint of iCharacter Ltd.

Copyright iCharacter Limited. All rights reserved. No part of this book may be reproduced in any form or by any electronic or mechanical means, including information storage and retrieval systems, without written permission from the publisher or author, except in the case of a reviewer, who may quote brief passages embodied in critical articles or in a review.

www.ingramcontent.com/pod-product-compliance
Lightning Source LLC
Chambersburg PA
CBHW040003080526
44586CB00027B/2864